Hollywood Portraits

MARLENE DIETRICH

Hollywood Portraits

MARLENE DIETRICH

Marie Cahill

Published by Magna Books
Magna Road
Wigston
Leicester LE8 2ZH

Produced by Bison Books Ltd.
Kimbolton House
117 A Fulham Rd.
London SW3 6RL

ISBN 1-85422-225-2

Printed in Hong Kong

All photos courtesy American Graphic Systems, except:
Brompton Photo Library 14, 15 (bottom), 17, 20, 21 (top), 30 (top), 71 (bottom), 80 (all), 92, 94 (top), 96 (top), 104, 107, 108 (top)

Page 1: When Dietrich arrived in Hollywood, she was advertised as 'the woman all women want to see.'
Page 2: Dietrich, early in her career.
Facing page: Elegant and enigmatic, Marlene Dietrich enthralled audiences for decades.

INTRODUCTION

Marlene. Her name says it all — glamour, beauty and, most of all, mystery. Even the year of her birth is a puzzle that the lady herself refuses to solve.

When Marlene Dietrich first arrived in Hollywood in 1930, it was generally believed that she had been born Maria Magdalena von Losch in Berlin in 1904, the daughter of Edouard von Losch, a cavalry lieutenant, and Wilhel-

Facing page: An early publicity still, before von Sternberg had completed his transformation of her into glamorous star.

Below: Marlene Dietrich at age 5.

mina Elisabeth Josephine Felsing. Years later, a birth certificate was discovered, revealing that her year of birth was 1901 and that von Losch was her stepfather. Her real father, Louis Erich Otto Dietrich, an officer in the Royal Prussian Police, had died when she was young. Von Losch himself was killed on the Russian front during World War I. Raised in an upper-middle class, conservative home, her home life emphasized the importance of duty and discipline—characteristics that would shape her acting career in the years to come.

Marlene's early aspirations looked toward a career as a concert violinist, but a wrist injury dashed those dreams. She then turned to acting, but after failing an audition with director Max Reinhardt she joined the chorus line of a touring musical revue. A year later, Marlene again auditioned for Reinhardt and this time was accepted for his drama school. She began appearing in small roles on stage and film. In 1923, Rudolf Sieber, a Czech production assist-

Above: Here we see something of the woman of von Sternberg's dreams. Contrast this photo with the one on the previous page.

ant, selected her for a supporting part, her biggest role to date, in the film **Tragodie der Liebe (Tragedy of Love)**. The following year, Sieber and Dietrich were married, and in 1925, their daughter, Maria—nicknamed Heidede—was born.

After playing a number of roles on the German stage and screen, Marlene was discovered by film director Josef von Sternberg, who cast her as Lola Lola, the seductive vamp of **The Blue Angel** (1930). The film was an immediate international success and marked the beginning of a five-year collaboration between von Sternberg and Dietrich. Leaving her husband and daughter behind, she went to Hollywood, where von Sternberg completed his transformation of the plump fräulein into a glamorous star—and his ideal of the perfect woman.

The six films that they worked on together in Hollywood—**Morocco** (1930), **Dishonored** (1931), **Blonde Venus** (1932), **Shanghai Express** (1932), **The Scarlet Empress** (1934) and **The Devil Is a Woman** (1935)—are considered

Above: Marlene with mentor Josef von Sternberg on the set of **Morocco** (1930), their first film in Hollywood.

to be the apex of von Sternberg's career.

Meanwhile, their screen collaboration had engendered rumors of a romantic liaison, and von Sternberg's wife sued Dietrich for alienation of her husband's affection. By this time, however, Dietrich's husband and daughter had joined her in Hollywood and she won the court case.

After **The Devil Is a Woman**, von Sternberg ended his relationship with Dietrich and left Paramount for Columbia. Studio heads at Paramount, disappointed with box office receipts from **The Devil Is a Woman**, did not object to von Sternberg's departure and assigned Dietrich to work with other directors. She still fascinated millions with her husky voice and raw sexuality, but by the late 1930s her career was declining. Labeled box office poison, she left Hollywood for two years, until Joe Pasternak of Universal offered her a part in **Destry Rides Again** (1939). The film resurrected her career and revealed a new Dietrich—a tough saloon hostess had replaced von Sternberg's *femme fatale*.

In 1937, while filming **Knight Without Armor** in England, she was approached by Nazi agents who tried to persuade her to return to Germany. Rumor has it that Hitler sent Joachim von Ribbentrop, the ambassador to England, as his personal emissary. When Dietrich refused Hitler's offer, her films were banned in Germany. Two years later she became an American citizen, and during World War II entertained US troops, participated in war bond efforts and made anti-Nazi broadcasts in German. Following the war, she was awarded the Medal of Freedom. France accorded her with a similar award, naming her a Chevalier of the French Legion of Honor.

A distinction of a far different sort came her way in 1948 when her daughter Maria had a son, and the media dubbed her 'the world's most glamorous grandmother.' Dietrich was devoted to her daughter and the two spent a great deal of time together. As for Dietrich's husband, the couple had been apart almost since Sieber's arrival in Hollywood. At first he had made an effort to be involved in the industry but soon gave up all pretense for chicken farming. Though they remained apart, they never divorced.

In the 1950s, Dietrich entered a new phase of her career as a recording star and cabaret performer. The legendary Dietrich was as well received in the clubs of Las Vegas and New York as she had been in Hollywood two decades before. Her popularity was universal, with performances in London, Paris, Moscow, Tel Aviv and even Berlin. Well into the 1970s she remained a symbol of glamour and mystery, and to this day is a Hollywood icon.

Facing page: Marlene Dietrich—the glamorous movie star.

MARLENE DIETRICH

Above: Marlene Dietrich as Lola Lola, the heartless cabaret singer in **The Blue Angel/Der Blue Engel** (1930), the film that catapulted her to international stardom. Although she had appeared in 17 previous films, she was an unknown actress until director Josef von Sternberg cast her as Lola Lola. When the film was completed, von Sternberg returned to Hollywood, bringing Marlene with him.

Facing page: Ten years after **The Blue Angel**, Marlene Dietrich starred in **Seven Sinners** (1940). The transformation to exotic *femme fatale* had long since been completed and her status as a legend was well in place.

Above: Posed seductively on a barrel in her top hat and garters, Lola Lola (Marlene Dietrich) embodied the decadence that was Berlin in the 1920s.

Facing page, above: Dietrich and Josef von Sternberg in Hollywood. Von Sternberg first saw Marlene Dietrich in *Two Neckties* on the Berlin stage and knew immediately that she was the woman to portray the erotic Lola Lola. Years later he recalled, 'Here was the face I sought, and so far as I could tell, a figure that did justice to it. Moreover, there was something else I had not sought, something that told me my search was over.'

Though she believed she was wrong for the part, Dietrich was a willing pupil. Indeed, her willingness to be dominated by him made the film a masterpiece and her a legend.

Facing page, below: Marlene and Emil Jannings as Professor Rath, the man who loses his soul through his desire for Lola. **The Blue Angel/Der Blue Engel** (1930) was Emil Jannings' talkie debut. Jannings was a highly regarded actor who had won the first-ever Academy Award for Best Actor, but his performance was overshadowed by that of Marlene Dietrich's.

Pictures

P1167-17

Above: For her first Hollywood film, Marlene was again cast as a nightclub singer in **Morocco** (1930). She is seen here with Paul Porcasi.

Morocco was the first of six Dietrich-von Sternberg collaborations for Paramount Pictures, and it was the beginning of von Sternberg's transformation of her. Prior to filming, he encouraged her to lose weight. Once filming began he, along with cameraman Lee Garmes, worked to find the best lighting for her. Lighting from above emphasized her cheekbones, while lighting from the front made her face look rounder, as in **The Blue Angel**. Von Sternberg also took dozen of takes to ensure that every word and inflection would be perfect.

Facing page: Once in Hollywood, Paramount tried to promote Dietrich as a Greta Garbo-type. However, Marlene's own distinctive personality shone through loud and clear, allowing Paramount executives to see that they had a gem of their own.

Above: In **Morocco** (1930), Marlene played Amy Jolly, a nightclub singer who falls in love with a womanizer in the Foreign Legion (Gary Cooper). In contrast to **The Blue Angel**, in which she played the heartbreaker, Cooper leaves Marlene at the conclusion of **Morocco**, only to be followed across the desert by Marlene, who has forsaken security in the name of love.

Facing page: A 1931 studio portrait of Marlene Dietrich. Studio portraits such as these were crucial to the process of becoming a star, for they appeared in fan magazines—the most effective means for luring fans into movie theaters. Studio portraits fit the magazine format better than the scene stills taken on the set after each scene. Consequently, each movie company installed a portrait studio to re-create the on-screen images. Soon the studio photographers were doing more than re-creating images; they were evolving their own approach and inventing the Hollywood glamour portrait.

Above: Marlene Dietrich and Gary Cooper in a scene from **Morocco** (1930). With her husband and daughter back in Germany, Marlene helped to overcome her homesickness by inserting personal belongings into the set of her films. The small Japanese doll in the right hand corner of the photo was one of her good luck charms.

Facing page, above: Von Sternberg wanted to show that Marlene's sexuality was derived from more than just her beautiful legs, so he dressed her in top hat and tails for a cabaret scene in **Morocco**.

Facing page, below: Marlene Dietrich with Maurice Chevalier and Gary Cooper. Almost overnight, Marlene popularized women wearing slacks.

Dietrich's second Hollywood film was **Dishonored** (1931), the saga of a prostitute-turned-spy. Marlene played the Mata Hari-type character, a spy with the code name X-27. Her exotic costumes included a leather aviatrix uniform and the Hermes Kit black chain outfit seen on *these pages*.

Her performance was met with critical acclaim. Richard Watts, Jr declared: 'She proves that her hasty rise to film celebrity was the result of neither luck, accident nor publicity.... Her almost lyrically ironic air of detachment and, to be as frank about it as possible, her physical appeal, make her one of the great personages of the local drama.' With only two American films to her credit, Marlene was a bona fide star, and, to the American public, an overnight star. American audiences had not witnessed her rise from bit player to second lead and ultimately to leading player.

When **Dishonored** was completed, Dietrich left for Berlin to visit her husband and daughter, bringing little Maria back to Hollywood with her. Her husband, Rudolf Sieber, soon joined them. In time, Sieber would go his own way. He and Marlene remained close, and on occasion they would spend brief periods of time together, but they never lived together again, nor did they ever divorce.

These pages: Generally regarded as the finest film von Sternberg and Dietrich made together, **Shanghai Express** (1932) distills the essence of the Dietrich persona—the woman of disrepute who transcends her past, attaining a higher moral plane. The striking portrait on the *facing page* was made by Don English.

Above: Marlene with Clive Brook, who played her former lover. After a separation of several years, they meet again on a train – the *Shanghai Express* – when it is hijacked by a Chinese warlord. Almost all the action in **Shanghai Express** (1932) takes place on board the train as it journeys from Peking to Shanghai.

Facing page: With **Shanghai Express**, Dietrich put an end to the comparisons to Greta Garbo. Her loveliness was all her own.

Overleaf: Marlene Dietrich and Clive Brook in a scene from **Shanghai Express**. It is in this film that she utters the immortal line to Clive Brook: 'It took more than one man to change my name to Shanghai Lily.'

Above: Dietrich adorned in feathers for **Shanghai Express** (1932). The film is noted for its exotic costumes and dazzling photography, for which Lee Garmes won an Academy Award.

Facing page: Dietrich as Shanghai Lily is both tough and vulnerable, sensuous and innocent. Marlene was a foundation upon which any and all emotion could be placed to be viewed with equal clarity.

Below: Dietrich as Shanghai Lily, with one of the Chinese rebels who have seized the train on which she was traveling.

Above: Though in real life Dietrich was a devoted mother, the image of Dietrich as a housewife in **Blonde Venus** (1932) took audiences by surprise. This was her first American film to cast her in a contemporary setting, and some critics felt that Dietrich was better suited to more exotic locales, such as we have seen in **Morocco** or **Shanghai Express**. However, as the photos on the next few pages reveal, **Blonde Venus** has its share of interesting venues.

Von Sternberg was once again the director, and it is interesting to note the parallels between Dietrich and her character, Helen Faraday, who pursues a career in entertainment while her husband is in Germany. Did von Sternberg see part of himself in the Cary Grant character—a man who becomes enchanted with Helen the first time he sees her perform?

Facing page: No one could use a cigarette and its attendant plume of smoke to evoke a mood like Dietrich could.

Above and facing page, above: Marlene Dietrich and her costar in **Blonde Venus** (1932), a young actor named Cary Grant. This role helped Grant on his way to becoming one of Hollywood's favorite romantic leads.

Grant played a dashing politician to Dietrich's housewife-turned-cabaret singer. After learning that the two are having an affair, Dietrich's husband, played by Herbert Marshall, has her son taken away from her, and she ends up in a shelter for women (*facing page, below*) where she vows to rise again...and in the next scene we find Dietrich the toast of Paris.

These pages: **Blonde Venus** (1932) features Dietrich's most unusual cabaret number—Hot Voodoo, which begins with Dietrich in a gorilla suit. A striptease reveals a curly, blonde Dietrich who sings:

Did you ever happen to hear of voodoo?
Hear it and you won't give a darn what you do!
Tomtoms put me under a cult of voodoo,
And the whole night long
I don't know the right from wrong.

During the Hot Voodoo scene, the camera—not Dietrich—moved, so as not to destroy the lighting effects carefully arranged behind her.

After **Blonde Venus**, Marlene Dietrich starred in **The Song of Songs** (1933), her first American film without Josef von Sternberg—and she was not happy about this turn of events. Only the threat of a lawsuit persuaded her to do the film. In von Sternberg's absence—and with his approval—Dietrich was directed by Rouben Mamoulian, who was noted for his lyrical style.

As the portraits on *these pages* reveal, Dietrich under Mamoulian's direction is stunningly beautiful, but the exotic allure that characterized her appearances in her films with von Sternberg is nowhere to be seen.

Above: In **The Song of Songs** (1933), Dietrich undergoes various transformations, from a peasant girl to an artist's model to a baroness. Lionel Atwell played her husband, Baron von Merzbach.

Facing page: Behind the scenes on the set of **The Song of Songs**. The shot *on top* shows her with British actor Brian Aherne, who was making his American screen debut. Aherne played the sculptor who makes Dietrich his model and lover.

MISS DIETRICH

Above: An on-set portrait of Marlene Dietrich wearing a Travis Banton gown in the final scene from **The Song of Songs**. Sources are divided on whether Marlene herself posed nude for the statues featured in the film.

Facing page: Marlene Dietrich in her baroness attire for **The Song of Songs**.

Many of Dietrich's films featured her in male attire: In **Morocco** and **Blonde Venus** she donned top hat and tails, while **Seven Sinners** saw her in a navy uniform. Off screen (*these pages*), Marlene often favored a mannish look, but what is remarkable is that such a look could convey tremendous sex appeal. The photo *above* shows Dietrich with her husband, Rudolf Sieber, and their daughter, Maria.

Above: Marlene Dietrich was reunited with Josef von Sternberg for **The Scarlet Empress** (1934), a lavish spectacle loosely based on the life of Catherine the Great. The most visually excessive of the films von Sternberg made with Dietrich, **The Scarlet Empress** was created with extravagant costumes, massive sets and von Sternberg's trademark use of veils, smoke and fog between subject and camera.

Facing page: A costume test portrait for **The Scarlet Empress**. For a black-and-white film especially, it is crucial to see how the color of the costume appears on film.

Above: **The Scarlet Empress** traces Catherine's evolution from a pretty, young Prussian girl to a powerful ruler.

In the film's early scenes, Catherine as a child was played by Marlene's nine-year-old daughter, Maria Sieber. New to the United States, Maria was just learning English and had only one line—which she recited perfectly and with much delight.

Facing page: The elaborate costumes of **The Scarlet Empress** included Travis Banton's military uniform for the Russian czarina. Banton designed the costumes for all the Dietrich-von Sternberg collaborations for Paramount and, in fact, built his reputation on his daring designs for Dietrich.

These pages: Marlene Dietrich as Catherine the Great in **The Scarlet Empress** (1934), with John Lodge, who played her lover. Von Sternberg had a very clear image of the man to play Catherine's lover — and none of Hollywood's leading men fit that image, so he chose Lodge, a newcomer to Hollywood. A lawyer with a degree from Harvard, Lodge had given up a successful law career in 1932 to pursue acting. **The Scarlet Empress** was the high point of his acting career. After World War II, he entered politics, serving in the House of Representatives, as Governor of Connecticut, and as US Ambassador to Spain and then Argentina.

Above: Again we see Marlene's incredible ability to portray any mood and emotion. Here she is shy and alluring...

...while in this photo she has the look of a woman brimming with self-assurance.

These pages: The Dietrich legend is as strong today as it was when these portraits were made in the early 1930s. Her name still evokes the image of the ultimate glamorous star: beautiful, sophisticated, aloof. Dietrich had it all. As her good friend Ernest Hemingway once remarked, 'If she had nothing but her voice, she could break your heart with it. But she also has that beautiful body and the timeless loveliness of her face.'

Above: Dietrich's next film was **The Devil Is a Woman** (1935), based on *The Woman and the Puppet* by Pierre Louÿs. Dietrich played Concha Perez.

Facing page: A candid behind-the-scenes photograph of Marlene Dietrich on the set of **The Devil Is a Woman** (1935). Even when taken by surprise, she provides a stunning subject for the camera.

Above: Dietrich in **The Devil Is a Woman** with Cesar Romero as Antonio, the man she loves and then leaves for a former lover.

Facing page: Set in Spain in 1890, **The Devil Is a Woman** (1935) gave costume designer Travis Banton the opportunity to dress Marlene Dietrich in extravagant Spanish gowns. Dietrich considered Banton's work for **The Devil Is a Woman** his 'crowning achievement,' and worked tirelessly by his side helping to create the costumes that fulfilled von Sternberg's vision. **The Devil Is a Woman** is her favorite film because it is so beautiful.

Above: Dietrich in **The Devil Is a Woman** (1935). As the final Dietrich-von Sternberg film, **The Devil Is a Woman** marked the end of an era. Leaving her behind, von Sternberg ended his association with Paramount and joined Columbia. From this point on, Dietrich's films would lack the exotic sensuality that had made her a legend. As she recalled in her memoirs, 'Josef von Sternberg's decision, against my will, to terminate our collaboration...marked for me the beginning of a long series of mediocre films.'

Facing page: Dietrich's character in **The Devil Is a Woman** worked in a cigarette factory, so she mastered the art of rolling cigarettes around a stick, and, as an added trick, she made the empty papers swirl around in front of the camera before she filled them with tobacco. One day at rehearsals she was unable to see the paper and the stick though they were right in front of her. Concerned that she didn't look Spanish, Marlene had obtained eye drops to dilate her pupils, making her eyes look black. The drops also affected her vision, much to the chagrin of von Sternberg, who insisted that he would handle the details of making her look the part.

These pages: Bedecked with a variety of flowers, combs, hats, veils and shawls, Dietrich played the part of a Spanish vamp to perfection in **The Devil Is a Woman** (1935). Outside of the United States, the film was distributed as **The Spanish Dancer**.

1983-114

Above: Marlene and Josef von Sternberg. Some critics have interpreted **The Devil Is a Woman** as a thinly veiled allegory of von Sternberg's relationship with his discovery. As evidence, they cite the resemblance between Marlene's costar Lionel Atwell (*below*) and von Sternberg.

Facing page: The incomparable Marlene.

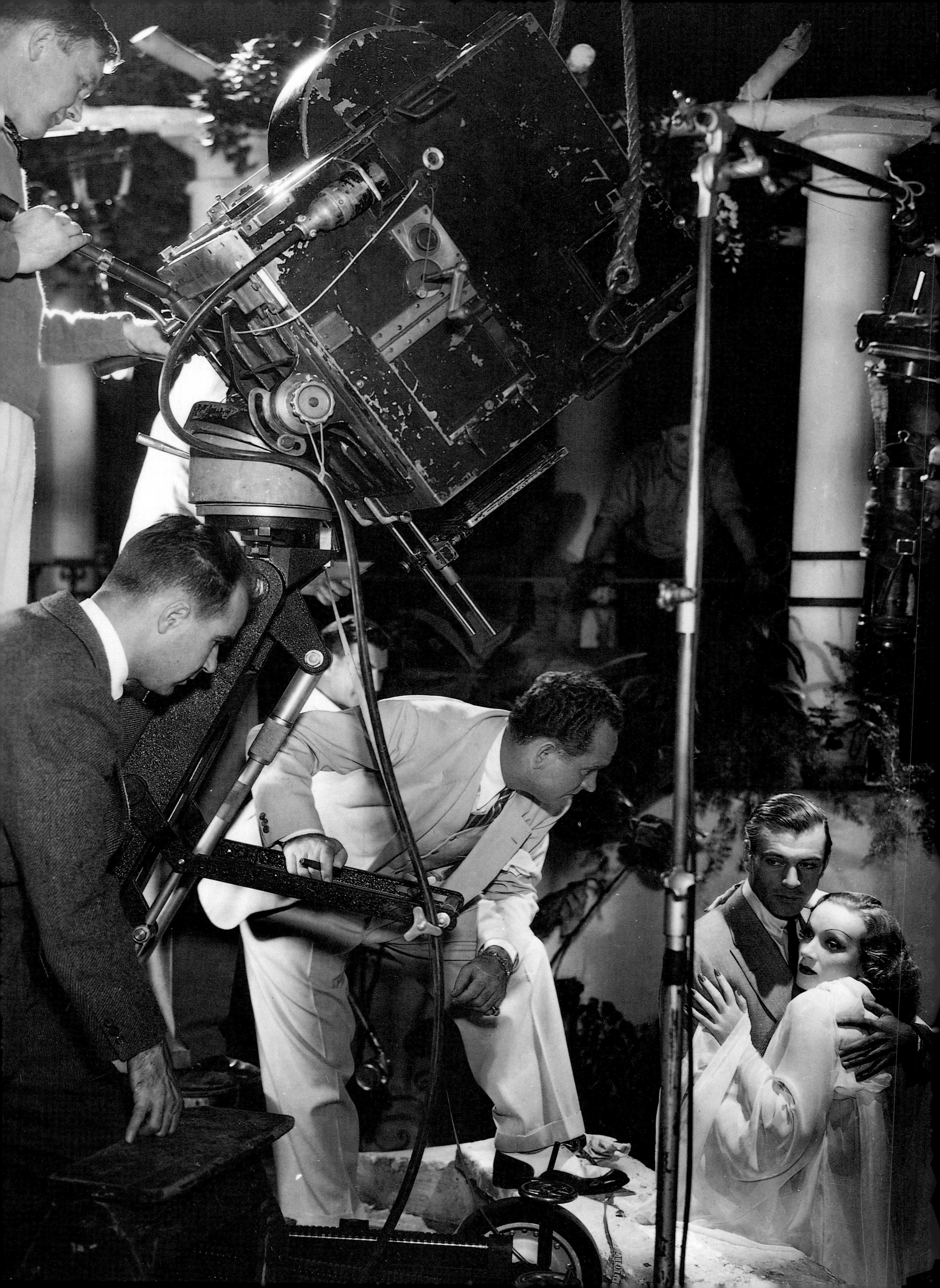

These pages: Dietrich's first film of the post-von Sternberg era was **Desire** (1935), with Gary Cooper (*above*) as her leading man and Frank Borzage directing (with cigar, *facing page*).

These pages: After **Desire** (1935), Dietrich's next film was to have been **I Loved a Soldier**, a remake of **Hotel Imperial**, a 1927 silent film with Pola Negri. She clashed with director Henry Hathaway and the film was never completed.

Charles Boyer was to have been her costar, and these two international stars did have the chance to appear together in Dietrich's next film, **The Garden of Allah** (1936).

Above: For **The Garden of Allah** (1936), Paramount loaned Dietrich to independent producer David O Selznick, who wanted to pay homage to **Morocco** with his own desert saga.

One of the first Technicolor films, **The Garden of Allah** is the story of a monk (Charles Boyer) who has left the monastery to find peace of mind. In the desert he meets Dietrich, who is involved in a soul-searching journey of her own. He breaks his vows and marries her, but ultimately returns to the monastery.

As a pioneer venture into the world of color, **The Garden of Allah** could have been a landmark film. Unfortunately, the dialogue was often insipid and kept the film from rising to a level of greatness. Dietrich, however, looked beautiful as usual.

Above: Dietrich with C Aubrey Smith in **The Garden of Allah**. While on the set, Dietrich did some movie making of her own. An amateur movie photographer for several years, she enjoyed recording life on the set. During rehearsals, she asked someone to film her scenes so that she would have a keepsake of her experience making the film.

Above and below: Dietrich played a countess in **Knight Without Armor** (1937), a melodrama set during the Russian Revolution.

Facing page: Though she wears her hat at a jaunty angle, her smile betrays a world-weary disdain.

Above: Marlene Dietrich, with Melvyn Douglas and Herbert Marshall in **Angel** (1937), an Ernst Lubitsch film about the mysterious wife of an English diplomat. A director renowned for his wit, Lubitsch missed the mark on **Angel**, and Dietrich was on her way to becoming box office poison.

Facing page: A still from **Angel**. Before **Angel**, Dietrich was one of the highest paid stars in Hollywood (she received close to $500,000 for **Knight Without Armor**), but when she received scathing reviews for her performance in **Angel**, she decided to leave Hollywood for an extended European vacation.

M.D-2

Above and below: Von Sternberg taught Dietrich to use lighting to her best advantage, as these publicity shots reveal.

Facing page: Marlene Dietrich returned to Hollywood as Frenchy in **Destry Rides Again** (1939).

These pages: While on vacation in the Riviera, Dietrich received an offer from producer Joe Pasternak of Universal Studios to star in a remake of the western **Destry Rides Again** (1939). Absent from Hollywood for close to two years, Dietrich was offered just a fraction of her previous salary—only $75,000. On the advice of her former mentor, Josef von Sternberg, she agreed to do the film.

Destry Rides Again showed a new Dietrich—earthy, and with a wonderful comedic flair—and though audiences were unprepared for this new persona, they loved her. The film was hailed as her comeback.

The still *above* shows Dietrich with Butterfly McQueen, best known for the role of Prissy in **Gone With the Wind**.

Facing page: As Frenchy, the madam of the Last Chance Saloon, Dietrich, who had once mesmerized audiences with her European sophistication, proved she was more than able to handle herself in a barroom brawl (*above and below*) with Una Merkel. Jimmy Stewart, who played the part of Destry, put out the fire.

M.II-13

Above: Frenchy (Marlene Dietrich) entertains the crowds at the Last Chance Saloon. In her extraordinary style, Dietrich sang the memorable 'See What the Boys in the Back Room Will Have.'

Facing page: It seems only fitting that Dietrich's first movie after becoming an American citizen would be the archetypal American film—a western. **Destry Rides Again** (1939) was directed by George Marshall.

Above: Joe Pasternak also produced Dietrich's next film, **Seven Sinners** (1940), a burlesque of the Sadie Thompson saga. Dietrich is seen here with John Wayne, who was on his way to becoming a legend himself.

Facing page: Donning male attire once again, Dietrich sang 'The Man in the Navy' in **Seven Sinners**.

Les

These pages: In 1941, Dietrich starred in **The Flame of New Orleans**, a period comedy set in old New Orleans. Directed by the French stylist René Clair, it was another Joe Pasternak production for Universal, but it lacked the sparkle of his two earlier Dietrich vehicles. The plot revolved around Dietrich's plan to marry a wealthy man. When she falls for a rogue, she changes her identity.

Her costars included Bruce Cabot, Roland Young and Mischa Auer.

Above: Whatever the setting, Marlene Dietrich was always the symbol of glamour, as in this scene still from **The Flame of New Orleans** (1941).

Facing page: Marlene as the sultry hostess of a clip joint in **Manpower** (1941).

Above: For **Manpower**, Dietrich was teamed with Edward G Robinson and George Raft. Raoul Walsh, who was known for his virile action dramas, directed the film.

Facing page: Marlene Dietrich became good friends with her **Manpower** costar, George Raft.

Above: In Mitchell Leisen's **The Lady is Willing** (1942), Marlene Dietrich played a Broadway star who decides to adopt a baby.

Facing page: While working on **The Spoilers** (1942), Dietrich ran into her old friend George Raft on the Universal lot.

These pages: Scenes from **The Spoilers** (1942), with John Wayne and Randolph Scott. The film was based on Rex Beach's novel about life in the Klondike around the turn-of-the-century.

These pages: Another Joe Pasternak production for Universal, **The Spoilers** (1942) tried to be a **Destry Rides Again** (1939) of the Far North.

1204-13

Above: Dietrich in World War II, ever glamorous, even in a soldier's uniform, and washing her hands in melted snow in a helmet (*below*) on a visit to the troops near Malmedy, Belgium.

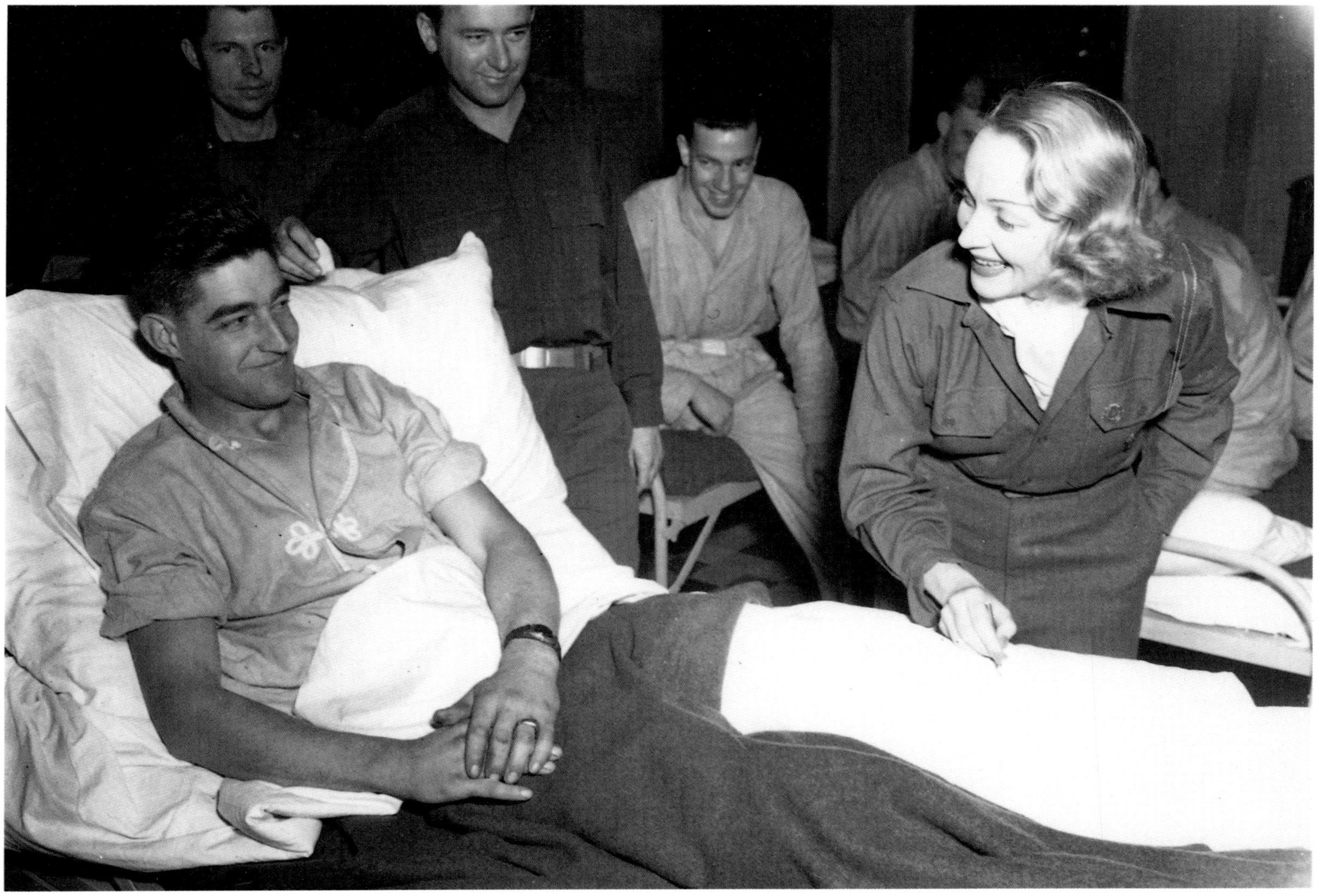

When World War II started, Dietrich began selling War Bonds across the United States. Wanting to do more in support of the war effort, she petitioned the USO (United Services Organization) to send her abroad. In April 1944, her wish was granted, and 'Colonel' Dietrich left for North Africa to entertain the troops.

Dietrich was devoted to the troops. After singing for them, she ate with them, joked with them and always visited the boys in the field hospitals, where she was invariably asked to sing 'See What the Boys in the Back Room Will Have.' In the photo *above*, Marlene Dietrich brightens the day of Tec 4 Earl E MacFarland of Cavider, Texas by signing his cast while he recuperates in a hospital in Belgium.

Above: Dietrich's first postwar film was Mitchell Leisen's **Golden Earrings** (1947), in which she played a Hungarian gypsy opposite Ray Milland.

The film lacked substance, and about the best thing that can be said is that it helped her ailing financial situation.

Facing page: A publicity portrait for **Golden Earrings**, her first film for Paramount in a decade.

Above: In 1950, Marlene Dietrich appeared in Alfred Hitchcock's **Stage Fright**. Each morning she appeared on the set to check the lighting or add finishing touches to her costume. Normally, Hitchcock, who was known for his autocratic approach to directing, would not have tolerated this sort of behavior. However, he saw that her recommendations did improve things and allowed her to be one of the few actors with whom he worked to offer creative advice.

Facing page: Cast as a world-famous actress, Dietrich's role in **Stage Fright** played on the real-life Dietrich legend.

SF-10

Above: In 1956, Marlene Dietrich made a cameo appearance in Michael Todd's **Around the World in 80 Days** as a San Francisco saloon keeper. She is seen here with David Niven and Frank Sinatra, who played the piano player.

Facing page: A publicity still for **Rancho Notorious** (1952), highlighting her famous legs. Another variation on the **Destry Rides Again** theme, **Rancho Notorious**, a mediocre film, is best known for the behind-the-scenes acrimony between Marlene and director Fritz Lang.

After the film, Dietrich divided her time between her nightclub engagements around the world and her daughter and grandchildren in Paris. From this point on, her film career included only one substantial role and a few cameo appearances.

These pages: Marlene Dietrich's last substantial film role was in Stanley Kramer's **Judgment at Nuremberg** (1961), a drama about the trial of Nazi war criminals, in which she played Frau Bertholt, the widow of a German officer.

Above and facing page, above: Dietrich's swan song on the screen was a brief appearance as a madam in **Just A Gigolo** (1978), a portrait of Berlin in the years following World War I.

Facing page, below: Though aging, Marlene Dietrich remains the eternal woman of mystery.

Filmography

Der Kleine Napoleon/The Little Napoleon (1923)
Tragödie Der Liebe/Tragedy of Love (1923)
Der Mensch am Wege/The Man at the Roadside (1923)
Der Spring ins Leben/Leap into Life (1924)
Die Freudlose Gasse/Joyless Street (1925)
Manon Lescaut (1926)
Eine Du Barry von Heute/A Modern Du Barry (1926)
Madame Wünsht Keine Kinder/ Madame Doesn't Want Children (1926)
Hopf Hoch, Charly!/Head Up, Charly! (1926)
Der Juxbaron/The Bogus Baron (1927)
Sein Grösster Bluff/His Greatest Bluff (1927)
Café Electric (1927)
Prinzessin Olala/Princess Olala (1928)
Ich Küsse Ihre Hand, Madame/I Kiss Your Hand, Madame
Die Frau, Nach Der Man Sich Sehnt/ The Woman One Longs For (1929)
Das Schiff Der Verloreenen Menschen/ Ship of Lost Souls (1929)
Gefahren Der Brautzeit/Dangers of the Engagement Period (1929)
Der Blaue Engel/The Blue Angel (1930)
Morocco (1930)
Dishonored (1931)
Shanghai Express (1932)
Blonde Venus (1932)
The Song of Songs (1933)
The Scarlet Empress (1934)
The Devil Is A Woman (1935)
Desire (1936)
The Garden of Allah (1936)
Knight Without Armor (1937)
Angel (1937)
Destry Rides Again (1939)
Seven Sinners (1940)
The Flame of New Orleans (1941)
Manpower (1941)
The Lady Is Willing (1942)
The Spoilers (1942)
Pittsburgh (1942)
Follow the Boys (1944)
Kismet (1944)
Martin Roumagnac (1946)
Golden Earrings (1947)
A Foreign Affair (1948)
Jigsaw (1949)
Stage Fright (1950)
No Highway in the Sky (1951)
Rancho Notorious (1952)
Around the World in 80 Days (1956)
The Monte Carlo Story (1957)
Witness for the Prosecution (1958)
Touch of Evil (1958)
Judgment at Nuremberg (1961)
The Black Fox (1962)
Paris When It Sizzles (1964)
Just A Gigolo (1978)

Index

Facing page: After her film career, Dietrich entertained audiences in nightclubs all over the world. Here, she is joined on stage by another legendary performer—Louis Armstrong.

Page 112: Hollywood's Golden Age may have faded, but Marlene Dietrich endures as a symbol of that magical time.